'Architecture aims at eternity.'

CHRISTOPHER WREN

In our busy, modern, throw-away world it is humbling to realize that more than three hundred years ago Wren's staggering output was quickly and precisely calculated without any of the aids which we should today find essential. Throughout the entire thirty-five years he spent working on the massive and splendid St. Paul's Cathedral, Wren was also responsible for the rebuilding of eighty-eight London churches, four royal palaces, university buildings in Oxford and Cambridge, royal hospitals at Greenwich and Chelsea, and other minor works. This short study places Wren firmly in the context of his time, and indicates how many major architectural projects were being simultaneously undertaken.

MICHAEL ST. JOHN PARKER

Contents

'That miracle of a youth.'

JOHN EVELYN on Wren

Above: *East Knoyle Church, where Wren's father was rector.*

Christopher Wren was born on 20 October, 1632, at East Knoyle in Wiltshire, where his father was rector. Young Christopher was a delicate child, but a determined one – as he doubtless had to be, in order to survive Westminster School (1641–46). In 1649 he went up to Wadham College, Oxford, where he quickly attracted attention as one *'who, when not yet sixteen years old, enriched astronomy, gnomonics, static and mechanics, by brilliant inventions, and from that time has contributed to enrich them, and in truth is one from whom I can, not vainly, look for great things.'* (William Oughtred, the most eminent mathematician of his day).

By the time that Wren went to university, he had already invented a mechanical weather recorder, a device for writing in the dark, and a deaf-and-dumb alphabet, and had written a treatise on spherical trigonometry. His activities at Oxford led him through such fields as anatomy, microscopy, astronomy, and various branches of mathematics. From 1653 to 1657 he studied as a Fellow at All Souls, and then was appointed Professor of Astronomy at Gresham College in the City of London. In

Right: *Part of Visscher's panoramic engraving of London before the Great Fire, showing Old St. Paul's rising above the cluttered streets of the mediaeval city.*

1661 he became Savilian Professor of Astronomy at Oxford, and one of the founding members of the Royal Society.

In his versatile pursuit of almost every branch of science and mathematics, Wren was not so much ahead of his time as among its pace-setters. What we now call the Scientific Revolution was in full swing, stimulated rather than inhibited by the political innovations and struggles of the period, and increasingly supplied with both openings and resources by the burgeoning commercial life of London. The physical, institutional and conceptual relics of the Middle Ages were tumbling down on every side in the second half of the seventeenth century and a new age was being born amid cries of joy and anguish. At the same time, and in fact as part of the same process, a new and passionate sense of national pride was being forged among the mingled disasters and triumphs of the French and Dutch Wars. Wren's talents fitted him ideally for such a time.

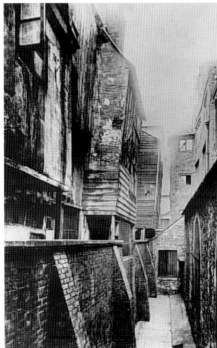

Above: *Christopher Wren exercised his youthful ingenuity by devising a deaf-and-dumb alphabet – perhaps more out of a desire to solve problems than for any philanthropic reason.*

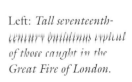

Left: *Tall seventeenth-century buildings typical of those caught in the Great Fire of London.*

'Our English Vitruvius, the Right Worshipful and Learned Sir Christopher Wren.'

ROBERT PLOT, writing of the Sheldonian Theatre

Wren's approach to architecture lay through the sciences and mathematics, particularly geometry and mechanics. This was the mode of the time: architecture was seen as a matter of producing solutions to practical problems, not yet as a form of self-expression. John Evelyn considered architecture 'the flower and crown as it were of all the sciences mathematical'.

It was doubly fitting, therefore, that Wren's first commission should have been for a learned society. In 1663 he was invited by his uncle, the Bishop of Ely, to produce a design for a chapel at Pembroke College, Cambridge. The result can fairly be described as a rather academic exercise, which owed much to Italian authorities. (The west front, in particular, was clearly modelled on a reconstruction by Sebastiano Serlio of a Roman

Below: The ruins of Old St. Paul's after the fire: an engraving by T. J. Wyck, showing part of Inigo Jones' west front.

For the present I behold St. Paul's Church, as one struck with the dead palsy on one side, the east part and choir thereof being quick and alive, well maintained and repaired, whilst the west part is ruinous and ready to fall down. Little hopes it will be repaired in its old decays, which is decayed in its new reparations, and being formerly an ornament is now an eyesore to the city; not to say unto the citizens in general, some being offended that it is in so bad, and others that it is in no worse condition.

FULLER's WORTHIES, 1662

THE ROYAL SOCIETY

The Royal Society was at the hub of the Scientific Revolution of the later seventeenth century. It grew out of gatherings of scientists, philosophers and savants who met at Gresham College in London as early as 1645, and subsequently in Oxford during the Civil War. The meetings were put on to a formal footing in London in 1660, by twelve leading figures including Christopher Wren, and it was incorporated as the Royal Society under the patronage of King Charles II in 1662.

The Society developed as a centre for scientific experiment, and a forum for a great range of ideas. Early members included Robert Boyle, the 'father of chemistry', William Petty, whose talents ranged from anatomy to economics, John Evelyn, the diarist and botanist, and John Locke, the philosopher. Members were required to use for their communications a compact and unembellished style which became the forerunner of modern scientific language.

temple at Tivoli, in Serlio's *Five Books of Architecture* of 1611.) But the building as a whole shows Wren sitting lightly to text-book rules about the correct combinations of classical motifs; he was more interested in the total geometry of the design.

This interest was taken much further in a second academic commission, this time for Oxford. Between 1664 and 1669, Wren designed a central assembly hall, or council building, for the University, the gift of Archbishop Sheldon – hence the Sheldonian Theatre. Once again, there is a Roman model – the theatre of Marcellus in Rome – but the freedom with which Wren adapted the formula can only be described as masterful. Roman theatres were open to the sky, but this would never do for the Oxford climate; so Wren designed a roof

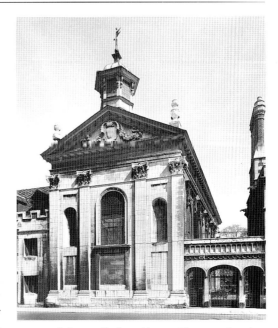

supported by a daring and brilliantly engineered system of dovetailed and braced trusses, to give a flat ceiling 70 feet wide and yet so immensely strong that the University printer could store his stock in the roof space.

Above: *The street façade of the chapel of Pembroke College, Cambridge, one of Wren's earliest architectural compositions.*

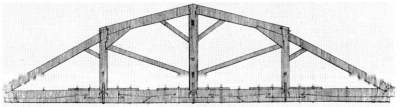

Left: *The curved north front of Wren's Sheldonian Theatre clearly indicates the geometrical subtlety of the construction within.*

Left: *The construction of the Sheldonian Theatre roof was a masterpiece of engineering which established Wren, at a stroke, among the leading talents of his time.*

The Great Fire ... 'London was, but is no more'

Below: *Leake's engraving of the survey of the ruins of the City of London, 1666.*

London at the time of Charles II's Restoration was still in many respects a mediaeval city, a dense huddle of timber-framed houses, threaded by tunnel-like alleyways and studded by scores of churches – all dominated by the vast, dilapidated bulk of Old St. Paul's. The Great Fire, which began on the night of 2 September 1666 and burned for three days, destroyed some three-quarters of this opulent ant-heap. It was an

September 2: This fatal night about ten, began that deplorable fire, neere Fish-streete in Lond: ... with my Wife and Sonn ... where we beheld that dismal speectaccle, the whole Citty in dreadfull flames neere the Water side ... *September 3*: The Fire having continud all this night (if I may call that night, which was as light as day for 10 miles round about after a dreadfull manner) ... I saw the whole South part of the Citty burning from Cheape side to the Thames, and all along Cornehill (for it likewise kindled back against the Wind, as well [as] forward) Tower-Streete, Fen-church-streete, Gracious Streete, and so along to Bainard Castle, and was now taking hold of St. Paules-Church, to which the Scaffalds contributed exceedingly: The Conflagration was so universal, and the people so astonish'd, that from the beginning (I know not by what desponding or fate), they hardly stirr'd to quench it, so as there was nothing heard or seene but crying out and lamentation, and running about like distracted creatures, without at all attempting to save even their goods; such a strange consternation there was upon them . . . behold the like, who now saw above ten thousand houses all in one flame, the noise and crakling and thunder of the impetuous flames, the shreeking of Women and children, the hurry of people, the fall of towers, houses and churches was like an hideous storme. London was, but is no more.

JOHN EVELYN, *Diary*

enormous disaster; but it struck a dynamic society that was confident of its ability to develop new forms on ancient foundations. The result was a new City. Modern London rose, Phoenix-like, from the ashes of 1666, and its gleaming feathers shone over the land.

Christopher Wren was one of those who leapt at the catastrophe as if it was an opportunity – indeed, for him, it was the opportunity of his lifetime. Perhaps as early as 11 September, he pressed on the King a first draft for a comprehensive scheme of rebuilding, which would have imposed a regular grid-plan of spacious streets and broad quays, pivoting on stately piazzas, and focused on monumental public buildings. Such a plan could never have become reality – it ignored all property rights, and would have required not only a despotic controlling will, but also unlimited resources to carry it to completion. It was a mere *jeu d'esprit* – but a very influential one, since it persuaded King Charles II that its brilliant young author was the man to supervise those parts of the rebuilding which could be undertaken by the Crown and the public authorities. It must have been on the strength of his Plan, rather than on any extensive evidence of architectural achievement, that Wren was appointed one of the three Royal Commissioners for the rebuilding. From that time until 1718, Wren was working more or less continuously, and more or less intensively, on the construction of the churches, public buildings, royal palaces and, above all, the great cathedral which effectively shaped the city.

Above: *Wren presenting his Plan for London to King Charles II perhaps a mere nine days after the fire began: the young architect showed opportunistic enterprise and political skill in putting himself forward at the crucial moment.*

Below: *Wren's Plan for London – not so much a working diagram as a career manifesto.*

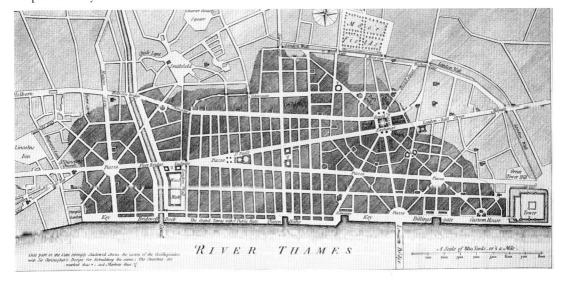

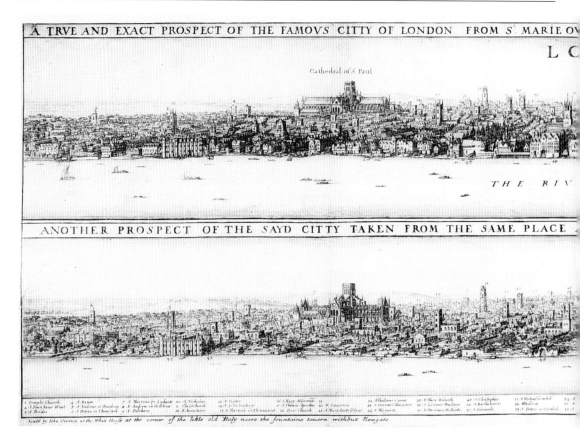

A TRVE AND EXACT PROSPECT OF THE FAMOVS CITTY OF LONDON FROM S. MARIE OV

L O

Cathedral of S. Paul

THE RIV

ANOTHER PROSPECT OF THE SAYD CITTY TAKEN FROM THE SAME PLACE

Above: *Wenceslaus Hollar's drawings of the City show the devastation of 1666.*

These Engins,(which are the best)to quench great Fires; are

Right: *A fire-engine made by John Keeling of London in a print of 1678.*

Sir Edwin Lutyens wrote in 1932 of Wren's achievement: '*There is no finer monument to his genius than the character that he gave to London*'. Sadly, much of that character has been destroyed since Lutyens wrote, often by the hands of civil and ecclesiastical vandals. Above all, the panoramic effects that Wren consciously strove to achieve have vanished irrevocably. The family chronicle *Parentalia* recalls Wren's intention to

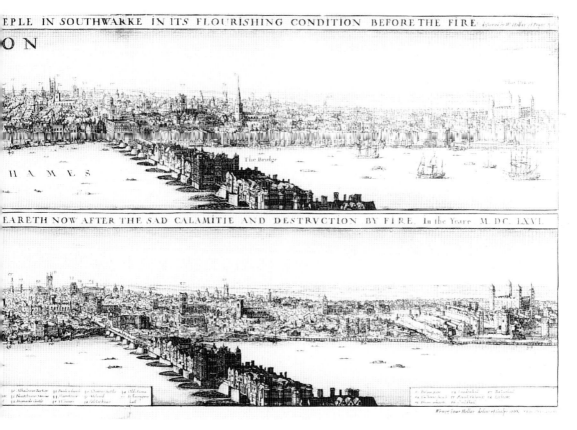

EPLE IN SOUTHWARKE IN ITS FLOURISHING CONDITION BEFORE THE FIRE

ON

THAMES

The Bridge

EARETH NOW AFTER THE SAD CALAMITIE AND DESTRUCTION BY FIRE In the Yeare M DC LXVI

rebuild '*all the Parish Churches in such a Manner as to be seen at the End of a Vista of Houses, and dispersed in such Distances from each other, as to appear neither too thick, nor thin in Prospect*', and Wren himself wrote in a Memorandum of 1711 of his desire for '*handsome spires, Lanterns, rising in good proportion above the neighbouring Houses*'. Many of the steeples have fallen; but those that remain no longer soar above a level tide of three-storey houses, rather, they drown in a stormy sea of building, of which the lowest trough is seven or eight storeys high. Wren's monument, in the sense of Lutyens' tribute, is no more.

Another monument remains, however – the Monument to the Great Fire, erected to Wren's design in 1671–76 on the site where the blaze is supposed to have started.

Sir William Holford's rebuilding of Paternoster Square and other buildings around St. Paul's after the Blitz was a failure, in both aesthetic and practical terms – an expression of post-war impoverishment and weariness, which is thrown into stark relief by the triumphant serenity of Wren's masterpiece. Plans are now being developed for a further attempt at providing the cathedral with an adequate setting.

Below: *The Monument was erected close to the spot in Pudding Lane where the Fire started.*

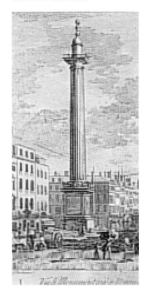

Oxford, Cambridge, London, Salisbury

Right: *Wren's work at Emmanuel College, Cambridge, shows a hint of French influence in the ambitious skyline and imperious massing of the façade.*

Below: *The Custom House, rebuilt by Wren in 1669 and burnt down again in 1718, was a strictly practical building which yet contrived to convey, in unmistakable terms, the mercantile greatness of the Port of London.*

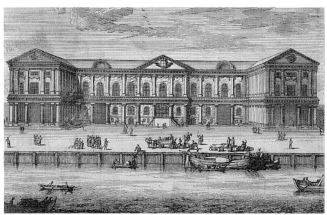

Between 1665 and 1668 Wren was again commissioned to design University buildings and a domestic range, one side of a courtyard, was built to his design for Trinity College, Oxford; it survives in an altered form which gives little impression of its original effect. Much the same can be said of a block designed for The Queen's College, Oxford, in 1671–74. An altogether more significant work, however, was the chapel and gallery range built for Emmanuel College, Cambridge, between 1668 and 1673 – though its design may date from the early 1660s. Here Wren combines external movement in the massing of the façade, and a proudly aspiring skyline, with an internal simplicity and economy which are largely unrelated to external appearances – a formula which he was to apply many times, in many variations, to the London churches.

Two larger public buildings of Wren's vanished completely quite early on – the large Custom House of 1669–71 in Thames Street, an imposing and handsome façade with projecting pavilions, all carried on open loggias, markedly Dutch in character, was destroyed in 1718, and Drury Lane Theatre was rebuilt in 1791. The remainder of Wren's London designs can conveniently be

SALISBURY CATHEDRAL

In 1669, Dr Christopher Wren was invited by the Bishop of Salisbury [Seth Ward] where he made a particular survey of the cathedral church. He was at least a weeke about it, and a curious discourse it was: it was not above two sheetes. Upon my writing the *Natural History of Wilts*, I had occasion to insert it there: I asked the Bishop for it, and he told me he had lent it, to whome he could not tell, and had no copy of it ... [Bishop Ward's] scattered papers I rescued from being used by the Cooke since his death; which was destinated with other good papers and letters to be put under pies.   JOHN AUBREY, *Brief Lives*

Wren's Notebook did survive and in it we can read his findings on Salisbury's Cathedral.

The Faults of the tower and steeple deserve the first consideration because it cannot ruine alone without drawing with it the roof and vaults of the church.

It stands upon 4 pillars like a table upon its 4 legs; 2 of these towards the West are sunk, but not equally. That to the South West is sunk 7 or

8 inches that to the North West half so much that this hath occasioned the leaning of the Tower and spire towards the South West ...

Therefore, for some years it should be often plumbed and a register kept; if the foundations settle no farther (as possibly it will not) it is undoubtedly secure enough. But if it moves the remedy will be to build up 8 bowes, from the walls of the navis. It is I confess, a chargeable, but I fear the only cure, for when so great a pile is once over poised, all bandages of iron will be but as packthred.

divided under the headings of the City Churches, St. Paul's Cathedral, and the Royal Works (which included the Royal Hospitals).

A great authority on Wren's work, Kerry Downes, remarks that 'Of all the categories of Wren's architecture, the parish churches are the most elusive and least understood, though they receive the most lip-service as treasures of Britain's historical and picturesque heritage.' The movement of population, changes in ecclesiastical fashions, the savagery of the Blitz and the philistinism of developers have combined to drain the churches of their functions, alter their appearance and furnishings, and wreak destruction on their fabrics. The result is that over half of the original fifty or so have gone for good, and the majority of the remainder have been more or less rebuilt, while the interior appearance of the most 'traditional' among the survivors owes more to Victorian taste than to Wren's own prescriptions. This process of attrition is the more regrettable, in that it was always the total effect, the cumulative value of the flock of churches clustered round St. Paul's, that constituted Wren's real achievement, rather than any perfection of detail in individual cases. Now that so many have gone, the original impact is correspondingly diminished – and it happens that some of the 'lost' churches were among the best.

Above: The church of St Dunstan-in-the-East was built 1670–71.

The City Churches 'are the most elusive and least understood'

KERRY DOWNES

Right: *The interior of St. Bride's, Fleet Street, before it was gutted in 1941.*

Far right: *St. Bride's was restored after the War. Bright, glorious, but not Wren!*

Below: *This plan shows the distribution of the Wren City Churches and towers that remain.*

Existing Churches

1 All Hallows-by-the-Tower
2 All Hallows-on-the-Wall
3 St. Andrew, Holborn
4 St. Andrew Undershaft
5 St. Andrew-by-the-Warbrobe
6 St. Anne and St. Agnes
7 St. Bartholomew-the-Great
8 St. Bartholomew-the-Less
9 St. Benet, Paul's Wharf
10 St. Botolph, Aldersgate
11 St. Botolph, Aldgate
12 St. Botolph without Bishopsgate
13 St. Bride's, Fleet Street
14 St. Clement, Eastcheap
15 St. Dunstan-in-the-West
16 St. Edmund, King and Martyr
17 St. Ethelburga, Bishopsgate
18 St. Giles', Cripplegate
19 St. Helen's, Bishopsgate
20 St. James, Garlickhythe
21 St. Katherine Cree
22 St. Lawrence Jewry
23 St. Magnus the Martyr
24 St. Margaret Lothbury
25 St. Margaret Pattens
26 St. Martin, Ludgate
27 St. Mary Abchurch

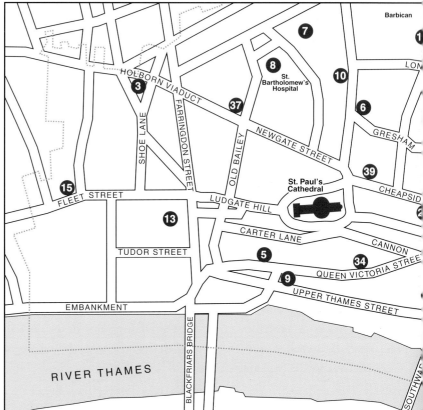

Wren is credited with building 51 churches in London after 1666 (88 had been destroyed in the Fire). The sheer scale of this programme ensured that his role was often more that of a consultant than a supervising architect in the fullest sense. The Vestry of the parish, acting as the clients, commissioned Wren to provide a design, usually employing whatever site – irregular, obscure, inaccessible though it might be – had been occupied by the mediaeval original. The details of the design were sometimes delegated to members of the talented team which Wren gathered around him for this purpose, including the versatile Robert Hooke and the even more brilliant Nicholas Hawksmoor. The actual execution was, likewise, a team effort, though one which became noticeably more accomplished as the years passed. The churches' furnishings and fittings were the responsibility principally of the Vestries, though Wren and his office gave advice in a good many cases. Finally, the financing of this whole gigantic undertaking of religious devotion and civic determination was based on a tax on coal.

Above: St. Peter Cornhill – one of only two Wren churches which still has screens separating the chancel from the nave.

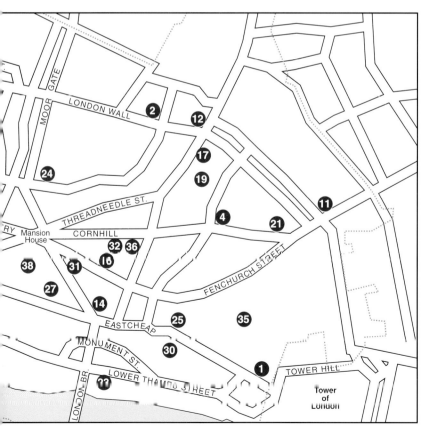

28 St. Mary Aldermary
29 St. Mary-le-Bow
30 St. Mary-at-Hill
31 St. Mary Woolnoth
32 St. Michael, Cornhill
33 St. Michael, Paternoster Royal
34 St. Nicholas, Cole Abbey
35 St. Olave, Hart Street
36 St. Peter, Cornhill
37 St. Sepulchre-without-Newgate
38 St. Stephen Walbrook
39 St. Vedast, Foster Lane

Towers Only Remaining
A　All Hallows-the-Great
B　All Hallows, Staining
C　St. Alban, Wood Street
D　St. Alphage, London Wall
E　St. Augustine-with-St. Faith
F　Christ Church, Newgate Street
G　St. Dunstan-in-the-East
H　St. Martin Orgar
J　St. Mary Somerset
K　St. Olave, Jewry

Above: *St. Mary-le-Bow was rebuilt in 1964, with little regard for the rationale of Wren's design, or for his colour-schemes; the result is uneasily assertive.*

There is no such thing as a standard Wren church. In fact, each of the City churches is unique, in plan and in elevation, and there can be no doubt that Wren found a lively satisfaction in the sheer variety of his designs. The largest group was formed on the single-cell pattern, like the college chapels Wren had built in Cambridge. Next in frequency came the basilican formula, with nave and aisles. Finally, there were some very irregular plans which owed everything to local requirements. There were flat ceilings, barrel vaults, and domes; many interiors were fitted with galleries, especially at the west end. The functional intention in every case was the creation of a preaching hall – not a space for sacramental worship. 'It is enough', wrote Wren, 'if they (Roman Catholics) hear the Murmur of the Mass, and see the Elevation of the Host, but ours are to be fitted for Auditories.'

The steeples, towers or domes of the City churches offer a whole field of study on their own. In their inexhaustible variety, they suggest every architectural mood from delicacy, through whimsicality to grandeur. Those closest to St. Paul's, such as St. Martin, Ludgate and Christ Church, Newgate Street, were clearly intended to make statements relative to the great dome of the cathedral itself. Others, such as St. Mary Abchurch or St. Edmund King and Martyr, are almost miniature in scale and intensely local in feeling. The most splendid of all, St. Mary-le-Bow and St. Bride's in Fleet Street, spring in glory to the clouds.

To discriminate, even among the survivors of Wren's fifty-odd churches, is so difficult as to be almost pointless. But the most subtle, sophisticated and successful of them all has yet to be mentioned – St. Stephen's, Walbrook, where Wren floated a dome over a complex space with a mastery that clearly foreshadows his crowning achievement at St Paul's. *'In this building especially, the geometry that Wren considered to be the basis of the whole world and the manifestation of its Creator, and the light that not only made visible the geometry but also itself represented the gift of Reason – light which was the first thing created by God – all fit into place like a mathematical solution. It is the strongest possible assertion of the true order of the universe'* (Downes).

Above: *The steeple of St. Mary-le-Bow, built 1670–80*

Left: *St. Stephen Walbrook is one of Wren's most masterly compositions, demonstrating his ability to achieve grand effects on a relatively small site. Sadly, as elsewhere, the removal of the original furnishings has destroyed some of the coherence of the design.*

St. Paul's Cathedral 'where 'stead of thinking of their God most men Forget His presence to remember Wren'

WILLIAM NOTY *c.* 1768

Above: *The church of St. Vedast was built in 1670–73 and the steeple added in 1694–97.*

Though Wren's works were many and various, St. Paul's was truly his masterpiece, the product of his concentrated energies and the sum of all his talents. Other buildings owe him their design, other projects benefited from his supervision, but St. Paul's was his lifework; it must have been a more than special moment when in 1710 his son, also called Christopher, ceremonially laid the last stone atop the great dome in his presence. We can follow the process of creation from the cathedral's first inception to its last adornment. Designs, building techniques, supplies of material,

Right: *An engraving of the west front of St. Paul's in 1713, shortly after the completion of Wren's grand design.*

wages and costs, furnishings and ornaments, fixtures and fittings, accidents and disputes – the records survive in minute detail, and all of them bear the mark of Wren's personality. His supervision was close and unremitting, but he was no aesthetic dictator, or tortured talent wrestling with a hostile world – rather, there is an impression of equable purposefulness fuelled by versatile enjoyment of successful practicality. St. Paul's is an achievement evolved rather than preconceived, coherent rather than logical, consistent rather than dogmatic, the expression of a very English personality. So much did Wren live his work at St. Paul's that we do not even know for certain where his family lodged all that time.

Above: *St. Paul's presides majestically over the panorama of London in this engraving of 1740.*

It was as early as 1661 that Wren was first invited to advise on the structural problems of Old St. Paul's, an invitation which turned into a formal appointment to a commission in 1663. Certain themes emerge early in his thinking about the cathedral; in May 1666, for example, he is found proposing a new crossing to be crowned by a dome – a form unknown in England at that time. Such adventurousness must have been stimulated, rather than daunted, by the sight of the ruins in the aftermath of the Fire; but the clergy of St. Paul's, by contrast, at first sought continuity, urging Wren to patch up at least part of the wreck for choir services. Only after falling masonry had demonstrated the impracticability of this approach did the authorities begin to think afresh.

SURVEYING OLD ST. PAUL'S 1666

[August] 27 I went to St. Paules Church in Lond: where with Dr. Wren, Mr. Prat, Mr. May, Mr. Tho: Chichley, Mr. Slingsby, the Bish: of Lond., the Deane of S. Paule, and severall expert Workmen, we went about, to survey the generall decays of that antient and venerable Church, and so set downe the particulars in writing, what was fit to be don, with the charge thereof: giving our opinion from article to article: We found the maine building to receede outward: It was Mr. Chichleys and Prats opinion that it had ben so built ab origine for an effect in Perspective, in reguard of the height; but I was with Dr. Wren quite of another judgement, as indeede ridiculous, and so we entered it: We plumbed the Uprights in severall places: When we came to the Steeple, it was deliberated whither it were not well enought to repaire it only upon its old foundation, with reversation to the 4 Pillars: This Mr. Chichley and Prat were also for; but we totaly rejected it and persisted that it requird a new foundation, not onely in reguard of the necessitie, but for that the shape of what stood was very meane, and we had a mind to built it with a noble Cupola, a forme of church building, not as yet knowne in England, but of wonderfull grace: for this purpose we offerd to bring in a draught and estimate, which (after much contest) was at least assented to, and that we should nominate a Committé of able Workemen to examine the present foundation: This concluded we drew all up in Writing, and so going with my L: Bishop to the Deanes, after a little refreshment, went home.

JOHN EVELYN, *Diary*

Right: *The Great Model of 1673 for St. Paul's can still be seen in the crypt of today's cathedral; the majesty of its design persuades the eye of the observer to forget considerations of scale.*

Above: *The church of St. Magnus the Martyr was being built (1671–76) when St. Paul's was started. The steeple was added in 1705.*

Wren's original design for a new St. Paul's, the First Model dating from 1669–70, advanced the dome formula which had been in his mind for three years or more. Other aspects of the plan, though significantly different from what was to follow, suggest that his architectural thinking was moving in markedly more spatial and less geometrical terms. The First Model evidently attracted a good deal of attention. But other, lesser works took priority for the time being – usefully, as it turned out, since they afforded Wren opportunities both to develop his ideas and to build teams of designers and craftsmen who were eventually to collaborate with him to unprecedentedly high standards on the cathedral project.

The next step was a reworking of the dome theme in the so-called 'Greek Cross Design' of 1672, which envisaged a centrally planned church on an heroically grand scale. This in turn developed into the 'Great Model', of 1673–74 – essentially the Greek Cross Design with a magnificent western portico. The Great Model, which still survives, is an extraordinary relic. Made of oak to a scale of half an inch to one foot – almost a miniature building – it is not only a triumph of the joiner's art (and originally also of the plasterer's and the painter's and the gilder's), but a stunning product of Wren's architectural imagination. If executed, it would have produced a building even mightier, even grander in the flow of its spaces than the one we now have. As the result of a single burst of inspiration, however, the Great Model version of St. Paul's might well have lacked the profound humanity of the long-matured reality.

Royal patronage was of central importance to Wren's success. His appointment as one of the three Royal Commissioners for rebuilding London in 1666 marked the effective start of his public career, and was followed by his selection – against intense competition – in 1669 as Surveyor-General of the King's Works. This brought him into close contact with the Court and the Treasury, at a time when architectural projects were seen as among the major concerns of government. The Office of Works, which Wren controlled until 1718, was responsible for the royal palaces and a formidable range of public buildings – so important a portfolio that the Earl of Shaftesbury, writing in 1712 as a political opponent of the regime, thought fit to complain that public architecture had suffered 'thro' several reigns … under the Hand of the one single Court-architect'.

The chief drawback of the Great Model in the eyes of those who examined it in 1674, however, was that it was based on a rationale that was unmistakably Renaissance in origin, as opposed to Gothic. This aroused anxieties; 'the Chapter, and some others of the Clergy thought the Model not enough of a Cathedral-fashion'. This was not mere conservatism; the resonances of papistry and autocracy conveyed by the Great Model may have been no part of Wren's intentions, but they were real enough to an informed contemporary audience.

The result was an episode which has caused much confusion. Wren drew up another scheme, markedly more Latinate in character and crowned with a dome so spiked as to resemble an onion-spire. This was deemed to satisfy traditionalist requirements, and received the Royal Warrant – but with the King's permission privately given to Wren to interpret it as he might think fit. The upshot, as executed over a period of thirty-five years, was a building close in spirit to the Great Model, though decisively Latin rather than Greek in plan. On the evidence of these changes, Wren has been accused of

The Office of Works, of which Wren now became head, consisted of the Surveyor and the Comptroller (Hugh May) and the King's Artisans – the Master Mason, the Master Carpenter, the Sergeant Plumber, with joiners, carvers, bricklayers and many others. There was also a Paymaster, a Clerk Engrosser, and a Purveyor who bought materials, whilst the main royal residences each had also their own Clerk of the Works.

Below: *St. Lawrence Jewry – the church of the Corporation of London, very splendid and very municipal after its post-blitz restoration. The vestry, appropriately, had the richest plasterwork in the City before its destruction.*

Right: *Trinity College Library, Cambridge: a palace of learning, but also a masterpiece of ingenuity. The floor level, slung between rather than resting on the supporting arches, was dictated by the levels in older adjoining buildings. Wren's work on Trinity College was begun shortly before his work on St. Paul's.*

indecisiveness, of politicking, and of deviousness; in reality, the process is better understood as demonstrating his inexhaustible willingness to explore different modes of thought, to apply varying logics, and to combine the results into a distinctive empirical whole.

By far the most important of Wren's university buildings, and designed concurrently with the first stages of St. Paul's, is the great library of Trinity College, Cambridge, which dates from 1676 to 1684 (shortly after he had been involved, in 1674, in the general supervision of a library gallery for Lincoln Cathedral, designed by John Tompson). Conceived, according to legend, by the powerful Master of Trinity, Dr Barrow, as a riposte to the university authorities for refusing his plans for a Cambridge equivalent to the Sheldonian, it exudes a stately air of austere command. The Palladian geometry of the façades shows Wren in what appears to be a composed,

Below: *The exteriors of Trinity College Library use themes first explored in Wren's Great Model for St. Paul's, and drawn in the last resort from Roman originals.*

High-Renaissance mode; and yet these are still façades, designed in the first case to close vistas with majestic finality, and related by ingenuity, rather than necessity, to the calm splendours (and studious practicalities) of the interior. The Trinity library conforms neither to Renaissance theory nor to Baroque passion; it is the product of Wren's own sublime pragmatism.

The first contracts for the work at St. Paul's were signed in June 1675. Between

PRACTICALITIES OF CONSTRUCTION

In October 1675 one hundred and twenty-four labourers were clearing the site of St. Paul's Cathedral. **'Seven hundred and fifty-three cartloads of rubbish had been carried away by January 1676, and the carting went on for many months more.** The best of the stone from Inigo Jones's old west end and transept fronts had to be sorted out and put aside for re-use. Timber had to be brought and worked into scaffolding and centering for arches. Bricks as well as lime and sand for mortar had to be brought to the site, and by the middle of 1676 new stone was also needed. This required special organization, for the work of Inigo Jones, both at the Banqueting House at Whitehall and at St. Paul's, had shown that stone from the Portland quarries in Dorset was the most durable in the damp, smoky London air. This had to be brought round to the Port of London by sea, unshipped below London Bridge, for its arches were low and narrow, brought further to Paul's Wharf in barges, and finally dragged up to the Cathedral. Arrangements for supervision, both in Dorset and in London, were to be a constant source of trouble. And on one occasion when England was at war with France, a ship carrying stone was captured, taken to Calais, and sold to a merchant of Rotterdam, and had to be bought back. Portland stone was used for all exterior work, but the accounts show that Reigate, Headington and Ketton stone was supplied for part of the interior.'

MARGARET WHINNEY, *Wren*

1675 and 1709 forty-one contracts in all were entered into, for masonry, supplies of stone, bricks, sand, lime and other materials, carpentry, joinery, plumbing, paving, iron-work, gilding and everything including the Great Organ. The grand total of expenditure has been calculated in the money of the time, as £846,214 12s.6d. – almost all of it provided by the Coal Dues.

Work was pressed ahead on as many fronts as possible, as near-simultaneously as possible. The foundations were laid in 1675, and the walls of the choir were first to rise. Contracts for the piers of the dome were placed in 1676, work began on the transepts in 1677 and on the nave in 1678. Construction of the west front began in 1684. Yet the uppermost works of both dome and west front were not settled, in either case, until twenty years after the ground-work had begun.

Below: The majestic scale of St. Paul's Choir simultaneously dignifies its human occupants and demonstrates their diminutiveness in the presence of the Almighty – an epitome, perhaps, of Wren's view of religion.

'Architecture', wrote Wren, 'aims at eternity'. He must surely have been powerfully conscious of his own good fortune in being able to take over thirty years in designing and creating one building – and yet to see it fully finished, and acclaimed as a symbol of its place and time.

Right: The last of Wren's university buildings was the upper part of the gatehouse at Christ Church, Oxford, which had been left unfinished by Cardinal Wolsey a century-and-a-half earlier. Here, in 1681/2 Wren created a belfry to fit above the two lower storeys of Tom Tower, whose flanking turrets are mainly of early sixteenth-century design. It was 'Gothick to agree with the Founders worke', but 'not continued soe busy as he began'. In fact, almost the only truly Gothic element in the design of Tom Tower is the repeatedly used ogee arch; but the result fits effortlessly into the Oxford setting.

CHRISTOPHER KEMPSTER
1625–1715

He came of a family of masons in Oxfordshire, an area with a particularly strong tradition of building in stone. The role of a master-mason at this time was to realise and execute the design of a building, which might come in almost any form, ranging from detailed drawings to the briefest statement of a general requirement. Thus while Kempster acted sometimes as Wren's effective site agent, he was also capable of producing his own accomplished designs; he is credited with the authorship of the County Hall in Abingdon, completed in 1680, a confidently imposing piece of civic architecture, and also with a splendidly pilastered and corniced house in Burford High Street. He played an important role in many of Wren's undertakings. Among the City churches, he was particularly closely involved with the creation of St. Stephen, Walbrook, and St. Martin, Ludgate; his name occurs frequently in the records of the building of St. Paul's, and he was active in working on the dome. Other employment with Wren included supervision of the work at Winchester Palace, and the erection of Tom Tower at Christ Church, Oxford.

INIGO JONES
1573–1652

The 'father' of classical architecture in England was Inigo Jones (1573–1652), whose designs for the Queen's House at Greenwich, the Banqueting House in Whitehall, and St. Paul's, Covent Garden, displayed a cool, assured mastery which won immediate admiration. So great was Jones' pre-eminence, that he used to be regarded as almost an isolated genius; in fact, he was the admitted leader of a considerable classical movement among architects and craftsmen, which continued through the troubles of the mid-seventeenth century and laid the foundations for the work of Christopher Wren and his contemporaries in the Restoration decades. These included, notably, Jones' pupil and nephew by marriage, John Webb (1611–72), whose work included the King Charles Building at Greenwich (1663–69), a part of a much larger baroque conception which was never executed, but which exercised considerable influence over Wren's subsequent work at Greenwich.

Above: *The south front of St. Paul's Cathedral. Wren borrowed freely from Inigo Jones' banqueting house – the two-storey design above a high basement, pilasters placed against a rusticated wall-face, a frieze on the line of the capital – but the scale, and the splendour, are all his own.*

Left: *One of the smallest, richest and most remarkable of Wren's city churches, St. Mary Abchurch, seen here beneath its exquisite painted dome.*

Above: *The church of St. Lawrence Jewry was built 1671–77.*

Questions about Wren's income are hard to answer simply. He received a salary, accommodation and expenses as Surveyor General, and salaries also for other positions such as the Surveyorships of Westminster Abbey and St. Paul's. But these were subject to political manipulation and could be complicated by the usual practices of office at that time, such as the employment of deputies. Wren also received fees, sometimes substantial, for specific pieces of work (£1,000 in 1693 for Chelsea Hospital, for example), and presents or 'reminders' which might be given in kind.

The wealth brought by professional success was hard earned through mastery of technicality. As early as May 1666 we find Wren claiming to have made advances in aspects of building construction, such that 'the

Right: *Canaletto's sweeping vista of Thamesside London, St. Paul's serene above all.*

raising of Materialls may yet be more facilitated so as to save in the lofty Fabricks very considerable part both of the Time and Labourers hire'. Complementary to the skills of the engineer, however, were those of the team-leader, and it was his success in assembling and managing his workforce for St. Paul's that turned Wren's vision into reality. Master masons such as Thomas and Edward Strong, Christopher Kempster and Joshua Marshall; stonecarvers such as Edward Pierce and Francis Bird; carpenters such as Richard Jennings; woodcarvers such as Grinling Gibbons and Jonathan Maine; ironworkers such as Jean Tijou and Thomas Robinson – all these, with their teams of followers and supporters, share credit for the great achievement. The meaning of their work perhaps comes home most of all to one who, starting from the choir with all its richness and intricacy, makes the long climb through the cyclopean structures of the dome, to emerge on the dizzy heights of the lantern, where the wavecrests of white Portland stone break for ever over the leaden slopes below – an unforgettable experience.

Above: *The church of St. Mary Aldermary was built in 1682 and the tower added 1701–04.*

'... and a little for pompe'.

CHRISTOPHER WREN, about his design for Greenwich Observatory.

The bellicose competitiveness that impelled dynastic rulers of the late seventeenth century into their murderously stately conflicts had the odd after-effect of instigating a matching competition in compassion. So the Stuarts, driven by emulation of Louis XIV, commissioned Wren to create splendid hospitals and retirement homes for the wounded and aged veterans of their army and navy, at Chelsea and Greenwich respectively.

With the work on St. Paul's well under way, work began at Chelsea in

Right: *The Royal Hospital, Chelsea: not so much a monument as an illustration of seventeenth-century warfare.*

1682 on a three-sided courtyard, facing southward to the River Thames. The central block houses a hall and chapel, behind a suitably military portico and a loggia under which the pensioners can enjoy the sun. The wings have all the regularity, and some of the crowded grimness, of a well-drilled battalion of infantry. This is architecture for soldiers – it should be remembered that its pensioner-inmates were still liable to be called up for active service, so this was a working barracks.

Above: *The church of St. Clement Danes was built 1680–82.*

GRINLING GIBBONS
1648–1721

Born in Rotterdam, he was one of a number of Dutch craftsmen who exercised considerable influence in England after the Restoration. Having been 'discovered' by John Evelyn, he gained royal patronage, and was regularly employed by the Board of Works. He specialised in carving decorative swags and pendants, especially of fruit and flowers, and particularly favoured lime wood because it allowed him to practise the extreme under-cutting of which he was a master. His work was never merely naturalistic, however; he had a flair for producing richly decorative effects within a larger scheme, and was highly valued by Wren, among other architects, for his ability to adorn an interior. He was a fast worker, and his carvings appear in many of the great buildings of the Restoration period – with the result that he has sometimes been credited with more than he actually did. He certainly worked at Windsor, Hampton Court, Kensington Palace and Whitehall; various city churches benefited from his hand, particularly St. Mary Abchurch where he executed the reredos, and he did much work for St. Paul's Cathedral, where the carving of the choir shows him at his best. Otherwise, Gibbons was extensively employed by the nobility to adorn their palaces, such as Burghley and Chatsworth.

It was one small part of Wren's role in that he was able to combine geniuses such as Gibbons into a working team.

Above: *The Thames at Greenwich, by Canaletto, in its day one of the noblest vistas in Europe.*

Greenwich presented more of a challenge to Wren's powers, in that the site was already partly occupied, by a small but highly esteemed building, the Queen's House, designed by the great Inigo Jones, and a much larger palace block by John Webb.

Wren's first offering, of 1694, was rejected, but work got under way in 1696, and proceeded rather spasmodically over the following decades – the Chapel Block was completed, to Wren's designs, as late as 1735.

The series of courtyards that retreat from the river front to the austere elegance of the Queen's House forms one of the noblest perspectives in England, and 'one of Wren's most important creations' (Sir John Summerson). Giant pairs of Corinthian columns, powerful rustication, and two elegantly balanced yet Baroquely eloquent domes move effortlessly between the flowing river and the slope of the hill behind. The little Observatory building, perched high above on the foundations of a Tudor fort, with which it sympathises in style, almost has the quality of a folly by contrast with the splendour beneath. The Painted Hall, started in 1703 and adorned by Sir James Thornhill, is one of the noblest of all memorials to England's maritime greatness.

Left: *The finest dining room in England? The Painted Hall of Greenwich Hospital, built by Wren and painted by Thornhill.*

Left: *Wren's extraordinary, almost instinctive virtuosity in echoing and shadowing the architecture of earlier ages is shown in his Greenwich Observatory.*

'The court style's Indian summer'.

KERRY DOWNES on Wren's surveyorship

Wren was an adaptable man, apparently equally acceptable to university academics and London merchants, vestry-men and aristocrats, Francophile Papists and Dutch Protestants. But in the end he was a king's man, for fifty years Surveyor-General of the King's Works, an office-holder under the Crown, and he might be surprised that we remember him as little as we do for his royal palaces – Hampton Court, Winchester, Whitehall and Kensington.

True, most of the Whitehall project remained a paper plan, Winchester was never fully finished and has long been demolished, and Hampton Court is only a part of what Wren drew. But perhaps it is the ideas, still more than the structures which embodied them, that are inaccessible to us today. We no longer understand the significance of King's Sides and Queen's Sides, the functions of grand staircases and privy closets, the meaning of state bedrooms and presence chambers – in short, we have lost the language of monarchy.

It might have turned out differently if Charles II had been able to indulge his architectural aspirations more fully in the 1670s – instead of

Below: Wren's designs for Winchester Palace would have given his royal master something like an English Versailles – but without much conviction, perhaps.

which he was compelled to concentrate on the rebuilding of London, and Wren with him. With more spacious times, however, Charles began to develop his 'Winchester project' – a scheme to turn the ancient capital into a royal retreat away from London, rather as the French kings had built Versailles at a distance from Paris. Winchester Palace was constructed rather hastily in 1683–85 on the site of the old Norman castle. A composition of receding courts focused on a dome, it was meant to be linked to the cathedral by a ceremonial avenue, and to be the crowning

glory of grand town plan. The nearly-completed shell was abandoned with melodramatic suddenness at the death of Charles II in 1685.

Above and left: *St. Paul's Cathedral Library: a secluded corner, rich in Gibbons' carving. All the time that Wren was designing an English Versailles for Charles II he was supervising work at St. Paul's, visiting the Dorset suppliers of stone and working with master craftsmen such as Grinling Gibbons.*

Above: *All of Whitehall Palace, apart from Inigo Jones' Banqueting House, was destroyed by fire in 1698. Wren produced two alternative schemes for its rebuilding but neither was carried out.*

Wren's first work at Whitehall palace was a chapel to accommodate James II's Roman Catholic worship. Built in 1685–87, to the scandal of Protestants, it was dismantled in 1688.

Wren designed some apartments for William's Queen Mary at Whitehall in 1691–93, but these were lost, with almost everything else except Inigo Jones' Banqueting House, by fire in 1698. The rebuilding which never happened could have given Europe one of its most grandiloquent Baroque compositions – and, with its formalised relation of monarch's palace to parliament's assembly hall, could have had far-reaching effects on England's constitutional development. But the exuberant freedom of Wren's drawings must have given cautious Dutch William more than enough excuse for failing to authorise them.

NICHOLAS HAWKSMOOR
1661–1736

Born in Nottinghamshire, Nicholas Hawksmoor came to London at the age of about eighteen and entered the service of Sir Christopher Wren as his 'domestic clerk'. He assisted Wren with the Chelsea Hospital project, can be found supervising the work at Winchester Palace in 1683, and was heavily involved with a variety of City churches. From 1689 onwards he was concerned with Hampton Court and Kensington Palace, and from 1691 he was Wren's principal assistant at St. Paul's. He carried out work also at Cambridge and Oxford, and became chief surveyor to Westminster Abbey in 1723. His London churches included Christ Church, Spitalfields, St. George-in-the-East (gutted in 1941), St. Anne, Limehouse, St. Mary Woolnoth, and St. George, Bloomsbury. He was largely responsible for the development of Wren's ideas at Greenwich, although the full grandeur of his scheme was never realised. His work in Oxford included the powerfully modelled south quadrangle of The Queen's College, and the soaring towers of All Souls' College. He made a notable contribution to the landscape of Castle Howard in Yorkshire, with his temple-like Mausoleum, but his most impressive work appears in his designs for the Palace of Whitehall – which was never built. The essence of Hawksmoor's work is his concern for architectural mass, which he deploys with confident enthusiasm, often using forms that seem to owe as much to Egypt or Mesopotamia as to Greece or Rome.

Opposite: *The splendours of St. Paul's provided the perfect setting for the Te Deums which celebrated English victories in the wars of Queen Anne against the despotism of Louis XIV; here Wren both served and created national greatness. At the same time his work for the King on Whitehall Palace (above) was to come to nothing.*

Hampton Court – a palace for William and Mary

Whereas King Charles II and the Great Fire of London had given Wren his great opportunity to prove his ability in ecclesiastical building, the accession of William III and Mary II in 1688 gave him fine opportunities in another direction. From his first visit to the old Tudor palace of Hampton Court in 1688, William was resolved to make it his principal seat, and from 1689 to 1702 Wren was busy with alterations and adaptations. Comprehensive redevelopment schemes were considered and rejected; half of the old, in the shape of Wolsey's entrance front, was retained, and half a new palace was built to face the gardens. Rectilinear, uniform, severely sumptuous, the new ranges are none the less full of

Left: *An eighteenth-century etching of Hampton Court Palace from the south-east.*

subtleties and complexities, some of them enforced by the site, and some resulting from the requirements of Wren's asthmatic patron, who wanted as few stairs as possible. This we may need to remind ourselves, was the man who strove unremittingly, not just to thwart, but to defeat the Sun King – there is no false humility here. What there is, very arguably, is evidence of expensive haste. Wren is working under pressure, perhaps more to the rule book than to his own judgement; the result is uneasy, heavy, lacking the serene poise of his best work.

Left: *St. Paul's Cathedral from the south-west: by the time Wren's work on Hampton Court Palace was completed, he would have another eight years of work to do on the Cathedral. Note the counterpoint to St. Paul's Dome provided by the church on the right.*

Above: *The Queen's drawing room at Hampton Court, rich and sumptuous like other grand rooms here, would have been part of a much more lavish building if Wren's original plan had been followed.*

Opposite: *The west front of St. Paul's Cathedral, the design of which was still being evolved during the years of Wren's work on Hampton Court. The relief above the pediment, by the sculptor Francis Bird, shows the conversion of St. Paul.*

SIR JOHN VANBRUGH
1664–1726

Vanbrugh was born just before Wren's great opportunity had come. Like Hawksmoor, he delighted in the rhythmic deployment of volume, but was happy to work on an even more expansive scale, and to far more elaborate plans. It is tempting to describe his work as characteristic of the gentleman-amateur, rather than the master-craftsman – and certainly he appears to have launched into architecture 'without thought or lecture', in the words of Dean Swift, in 1699 at the age of thirty-five, when he designed Castle Howard for the Earl of Carlisle. He had been born in London, the son of a wealthy sugar merchant, and had pursued careers as a soldier and a dramatist before turning to architecture. His success at Castle Howard led to his appointment as Comptroller of the Royal Works in 1702, and a series of rather incongruous appointments as a Herald. His principal work and greatest triumph was the creation of Blenheim Palace, from 1705 onwards, as a celebration of Marlborough's victory over the armies of Louis XIV; the result was a baroque statement of a scale and force unrivalled in England. Most of Vanbrugh's other works were great country houses or palaces. All are marked by force and originality, and when relieved of any restraints of scale, as at Castle Howard and Blenheim, his style becomes truly imperial.

Above: *The south front of Hampton Court Palace marches inexorably across the Thames-side plain – 'a design of stolid, prosaic massiveness'.*

Opposite: *The construction of the dome of St. Paul's was a masterpiece of engineering ingenuity, which made possible a whole series of interior and exterior architectural effects. The final design was evolved about 1704, not long after Wren's work on Hampton Court, Kensington Palace and Greenwich Hospital was finished, and when work on repairs to Westminster Abbey was still in progress.*

JEAN TIJOU
fl. 1689–1712

A French iron-worker, whose talent for florid yet disciplined work happily matched that of Grinling Gibbons in wood, and provided an essential element in many of Wren's compositions. His screens of wrought iron, lavishly embellished with arabesques and leaf-forms, often richly gilded, define spaces without entirely obscuring the view, thus adding to rather than reducing the dimensions of the enclosure. Tijou's handling of iron was wonderfully fluent, yet always powerful – the essential strength of the metal is always in evidence.

His work is to be found at Hampton Court and Kensington Palace, as well as in the choir of St. Paul's Cathedral, and in a number of City churches such as St. Andrew Undershaft, St. Benet's, Paul's Wharf, and St. Alfege's, Greenwich.

Kensington Palace – 'compact seventeenth-century house, ripe for enlargement'

Below: *Kensington Palace shows Wren at his most domestic and improvisatory, with results that charm us today.*

In 1688 William III bought Nottingham House and ordered Wren to enlarge it. It was to be the London royal residence, whilst Hampton Court, then in open country, would be the country residence where the King could indulge his passion for hunting. Haste was a factor at Kensington (parts of the work fell down during construction both here and at Hampton Court; the King accepted that he was pressing the masons to go faster than they should), but the job itself placed fewer strains on the designer. This 'palace in a garden', bought as an occasional retreat from Whitehall, was extended between 1689 and 1702 in a largely domestic style. If Wren had developed a country house practice, as his designs for Tring Manor (1687–90) and Winslow Hall (1699–1702) suggest that he might have done, it could have started with Kensington.

Left: *The Banqueting House at Hampton Court. In all of Wren's work here, the craftsmanship is of the highest quality in every detail. Many of the great rooms have coved ceilings rising above them, which are richly painted and decorated.*

Above: *Christ Church, Newgate Street, built 1677–87, only the tower now remains (1704).*

Left: *The south west tower of St. Paul's, showing Wren at his most baroque, with all the originality of maturity. One drawing for the west towers, partly at least in Wren's own hand, is dated 'February 25th, 1703-4', which was not very long after his work on Kensington Palace had finished.*

'... haveing worn out (by God's mercy) a long life in the Royal Service, and haveing made some Figure in the World ...'

Sir Christopher Wren, 21 April 1718

Wren's was a life crowded with professional business, yet he never seems to have been overborne with work. More than anything, he appears as a man doing always what he enjoyed most, namely solving problems creatively. Work came his way because he could do it, rather than because he greedily sought for it; office, similarly; honours, apart from his knighthood, awarded in 1673, hardly at all. He was no traveller – one expedition to France in 1665/6 was the limit of his adventuring abroad, and after 1666 he rarely even left London. He played a part in public life, as a member of the Council of the Hudson's Bay Company, as MP successively for Plympton and Weymouth, and as President of the Royal Society in 1681–83. He was never far from the centre of affairs, though men of lesser talent struggled far harder to assert themselves.

Below: By the early eighteenth-century coffee drinking was firmly established as a social habit, especially amongst learned gentlemen and the literati.

Wren seems to have been something of a foiled family man: married twice, but deprived by death of both his wives, his eldest son and a much-loved daughter, Jane, who died in 1703 at the age of twenty-six. His first marriage, to Faith Coghill, daughter of Sir Thomas Coghill, lasted from 1669 to 1675, his second, to Jane Fitzwilliam, daughter of the second

**SI
MOMENTUM
REQUIRIS
CIRCUMSPICE**

**If you require
a monument, look
about you.**

*The epitaph on Wren's
grave in the crypt of
St. Paul's.*

Baron Fitzwilliam, from 1677 to 1679. Both wives died shortly after giving birth.

In his prime, he figures in diaries such as Hooke's and Evelyn's as sociable, talkative, a coffee-drinker and a walker. Later, according to his son, 'Free from Worldly Affairs, he passed the greatest part of the last following Years of his Life in Contemplation and Studies, principally in the Consolation of the Holy Scriptures: Cheerful in Solitude ... Though Time had enfeebled his Limbs (which was his chief ailment), yet it had little influence on the Vigour of his Mind, which continued, with a Vivacity rarely found at that Age ... His great Humanity appeared to the last, in Benevolence and Complacency free from all Moroseness in Behaviour and Aspect.'

Wren outlived his friends and experienced the rejection that comes the way of all who outlast the days of their power. But the last of his steeples, St. Stephen Walbrook, was finished only six years before he died in his chair at his home in St. James' (25 February 1723), aged 91. His last journey to St. Paul's was marked by 'Great Funeral State and Solemnity', but he was buried in characteristic simplicity beneath a plain black slab in the crypt of his great cathedral.

Above: *The steeple of St. James, Garlickhythe (1676–82), was completed in 1717.*

Chronology

1632	20 October Christopher Wren born.
1646–49	In London.
c 1649	Entered at Wadham College, Oxford, as a Gentleman Commoner.
1651	BA degree.
1653	MA degree.
1653–57	Fellow of All Souls College, Oxford.
1654	Meets John Evelyn for the first time.
1657	Professor of Astronomy, Gresham College, London.
1658	Wren's father dies.
1661	Savilian Professor of Astronomy at Oxford; receives the degree of DCL at both Oxford and Cambridge; Foundation Member of The Royal Society.
1663	Member of the Commission for repairing St. Paul's Cathedral.
1663–65	Invited by his uncle, the Bishop of Ely, to design the Chapel of Pembroke College, Cambridge.
1664–69	The Sheldonian Theatre, Oxford.
1665–66	Goes to Paris 'to survey the most esteem'd Fabricks ...'; meets the Italian sculptor, Bernini.
1666	Submits to Charles II a plan for rebuilding London after the Great Fire; October, appointed member of the Commission for the rebuilding of the City.
1668	Reports to Dr Seth Ward on the structure of Salisbury Cathedral.
1668–73	Emmanuel College Chapel, Cambridge.
1669	Appointed Surveyor of the King's Works; Marries Faith Coghill at the Temple Church, London.
1669–74	The Custom House, London.
1670–71	St. Dunstan-in-the-East.
1670–73	St. Vedast, Foster Lane.
1670–76	St. Mary at Hill, Thames Street.
1670–79	St. Edmund King and Martyr.
1670–80	St. Mary-le-Bow, Cheapside.

St. Swithin's Church.

St. Andrew-by-the-Wardrobe.

1670–84	St. Bride, Fleet Street.
1671–76	St. Magnus Martyr, Lower Thames Street.
1671–76	The Monument.
1671–77	St. Lawrence, Jewry.
1671–77	St. Nicholas, Cole Abbey.
1672–79	St. Stephen, Walbrook.
1672	Eldest son, Gilbert, born. (d. March 1674).
1673	20 November Wren knighted at Whitehall by King Charles II; the Great Model of St. Paul's prepared.
1675	The Royal Observatory, Greenwich; son, Christopher, born; foundation stone of St. Paul's laid; Lady Wren dies.
1676–83	St. James, Garlickhythe.

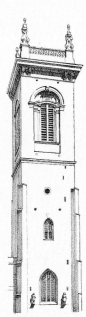

St. Andrew's Church.

St. Bride.

1674–84	Trinity College Library, Cambridge.
1677	Marries Jane Fitzwilliam at the Chapel Royal at Whitehall; November, Jane Wren born.
1677–80	St. Anne and St. Agnes, Gresham Street.
1677–83	St. Benet, Paul's Wharf.
1677 84	St. Martin, Ludgate.
1677–85	St. Swithin, Cannon Street.
1677–87	Christ Church, Newgate Street.
1678–82	St. Antholin, Watling Street.
1679	Son, William, born; Lady Wren dies.
1680–82	St. Clement Danes.
1680–86	St. Anne, Soho.
1681–82	Tom Tower, Christ Church, Oxford.
1681 83	President of The Royal Society.
1681–86	St. Mary Abchurch.

1682–84	St. James's Piccadilly.
1682–91	Chelsea Hospital.
1683–85	Winchester Palace.
1685	Returned to Parliament for the borough of Plympton, Devon.
1685–87	Whitehall Palace, Chapel and Privy Gallery.
1689–1702	Hampton Court.
1689–1702	Kensington Palace.
1691–93	Whitehall Palace, apartments for Queen Mary II.
1694–97	St. Vedast, Foster Lane, Steeple.
1698	Whitehall Palace, rebuilding schemes after fire.
1698–1722	Repairs to Westminster Abbey.
1701–03	St. Bride, Fleet Street, Steeple.
1703	Daughter, Jane, dies.
1704	Christ Church, Newgate Street, Steeple.
1705	St. Magnus Martyr, London Bridge, Steeple.
c 1708	St. Edmund King and Martyr, Steeple.
1709–11	Marlborough House, St. James's.
1710	Son, Christopher, lays last stone of the lantern above the Dome of St. Paul's in the presence of his father and the master-masons.
1713	St. Michael, Paternoster Royal, Steeple completed.
1714–17	St. James, Garlickhythe, Steeple.
1717	St. Stephen, Walbrook, Steeple.
1718	26 April. Patent as Surveyor of the King's works revoked in favour of William Benson.
1723	25 February. Dies at his house in St. James's Street; buried near his daughter Jane in the SE crypt of St. Paul's, aged 91 years.
1750	*Parentalia or Memoirs of the Family of the Wrens*, published by grandson, Stephen Wren, from a compilation by his son, Christopher.

Events and Personalities 1632–1723 of which Wren would have been aware

1642	Galileo died
1642	First Civil War began
1648	Second Civil War began
1649	Charles I executed
1652	Inigo Jones died
1658	Oliver Cromwell died
1659	Pepys began diary
1660	Restoration of Charles II
1661	Boyle's *Sceptical Chemist*
1662	Royal Society founded
	Versailles begun
1663	First Turnpike Act
	Guineas first minted
	Leibniz *De principis individii*
1665	Great Plague of London
1667	New Amsterdam becomes New York
	Milton *Paradise Lost*
1668	Leeuwenhoek discovers red blood corpuscles
1669	Rembrandt died
1670	Dryden – Poet Laureate
1672	Newton discovers laws of gravitation
1673	Huyghens determines centrifugal force
1675	Leibniz invents differential calculus
1676	Wiseman inaugurates modern surgery
1678	Titus Oates – 'Popish Plot'
	Bunyan *Pilgrim's Progress*

1679	Habeas Corpus Act
	'Whig' and 'Tory' names in use
1680	Penny Post in London
	Purcell *Dido and Aeneas*
1683	Rye House Plot
1685	Charles II succeeded by James II
	Monmouth Rebellion
	Judge Jeffreys – 'Bloody Assizes'
	Flight of Huguenots
1687	Newton's *Principia*
1688	Glorious Revolution
1689	James II succeeded by William III and Mary II
	Siege of Londonderry
	Battle of Killiecrankie
	Locke *On Civil Government*
1690	Battle of the Boyne
1691	Purcell *King Arthur*
1692	Glencoe Massacre
1694	Queen Mary died
	Bank of England established
1695	Purcell died
	End of press censorship in England
1698	Charter for New East India Co.
	Eddystone Lighthouse built
1702	William III succeeded by Queen Anne
1706	John Evelyn died
1701–14	War of Spanish Succession

Literary figures in Wren's later life include:

Defoe
Swift
Addison
Pope
Farquhar

Composers in Wren's life include:
Purcell
Handel
Vivaldi

Playwrights in Wren's life include:
Otway
Wycherley
Etherege
Congreve
Vanbrugh
Farquhar
Molière
Corneille
Racine

Although many events took place between 1713 and 1723 they mattered hardly more to Wren than he mattered to them.

Bibliography

G. Beard, *The Work of Christopher Wren* (Nicholson, 1982).

G. Beard, *Craftsmen and Interior Decoration in England, 1660–1820* Holmes & Meier, 1981).

K. Downes, *English Baroque Architecture* (A. Zwemmer, 1966).

K. Downes, *Sir Christopher Wren, The Design of St. Paul's Cathedral* (Trefoil Publications, 1988).

C. Hibbert, *London's Churches* (Macdonald, 1988).

P. Jeffrey, *City Churches of Sir Christopher Wren* (Hambledon Press, 1966).

J. Summerson, *Architecture in Britain, 1530–1830* (Yale University Press, 1993).

M. Whinney, *Wren* (Thames and Hudson, 1971).

G. Worsley, *Classical Architecture in Britain, The Heroic Age* (Yale University Press, 1995).

Acknowledgements

All photographs in this book are © A.F. Kersting ABIPP FRPS, except for the following, for the use of which the publishers gratefully thank:

All Souls College, Oxford, p.32;

British Architectural Library, p.3 right, p.5 bottom;

British Library, p.2 right (162.0.1);

Guildhall Art Library, p.3 left, p.4, p.6, p.8 top, p.16;

Historic Royal Palaces: Crown Copyright, p.38 top;

Mary Evans Picture Library, p.7, p.9, p.10 bottom, p.17, p.35 top, p.42;

J. Milner (1798), p.30;

Museum of London, p.8 bottom;

National Maritime Museum, p.28;

Oxford Picture Library, p.22 top;

Royal Collection, p.24;

Royal Society, front cover;

Philip Way Photography, p.18;

Kim Williams Photography, p.35 bottom.

Cover border by Andrew Stewart Jamieson

Line drawings by John Fuller

Text © Michael St. John Parker

Edited by Jane Drake

Design © Adrian Hodgkins Design

Typesetting and map work by White Horse Graphics

Published by Wessex Books 1998

Printed by Brunton Publications

ISBN 0 9529619 8 9